Grandma's Silver Series

Hello Mr. Spider!

by Diana Holt

illustrated by Josey Wawasniak

Order this book online at www.trafford.com
or email orders@trafford.com

Most Trafford titles are also available at major online book retailers.

 **Trafford**
PUBLISHING® www.trafford.com

North America & international
toll-free: 1 888 232 4444 (USA & Canada)
fax: 812 355 4082

Our mission is to efficiently provide the world's finest, most comprehensive book publishing service, enabling every author to experience success. To find out how to publish your book, your way, and have it available worldwide, visit us online at www.trafford.com

Because of the dynamic nature of the Internet, any web addresses or links contained in this book may have changed since publication and may no longer be valid. The views expressed in this work are solely those of the author and do not necessarily reflect the views of the publisher, and the publisher hereby disclaims any responsibility for them.

Any people depicted in stock imagery provided by Getty Images are models, and such images are being used for illustrative purposes only.
Certain stock imagery © Getty Images.

ISBN: 978-1-4251-2006-1 (sc)

Print information available on the last page.

Trafford rev.03/09/2020

I would like to dedicate this book firstly to my children,

Don, Randy and Tim

They have been with me through thick and thin, and have shared all phases and challenges with me. Thank you boys, I love you!!

Secondly, to all of my

Grandchildren and Great Grandchildren

who have given me more joy, fun and memorable moments in my life than they know. They have taught me to love, laugh hard and often, and to find delight in the simplest of things.

Thank You
to Josey Wawasniak
for the splendid illustrations.

A Special Thank You
to my many friends
for their endless continual encouragement.

Thank You to God
for being with me throughout my life, and never giving up on me.
My work would never have been completed without God's help.

HELLO MR. SPIDER

We were visiting at Grandma and Grandpa's house one day. I was in the Dining Room. I looked up and on the chandelier there was a huge spider and a web.

I shouted, "hurry Grandma, come quickly, there's a humongous spider on your chandelier!!"

Grandma came right away. She brought a piece of paper towel with her.

"Why do you have the paper towel? What are you going to do with it?"

Grandma carefully cradled the spider in the paper towel and put it outside.

I said, "Goodbye, Mr. Spider. So Long!"

"Why did you do that, Grandma?"

"Because", Grandma answered, "spiders are good creatures to have around, especially outside".

"Why, Grandma", I asked.

Grandma told me that spiders catch harmful insects and they **Do Not** eat plants.

"Then why put him outside?"

"I don't like webs in the house, because dust sticks to them and besides there are more bugs for the spider outside."

"So why do spiders catch insects?" I asked.

"Because they eat them to live", replied Grandma.

"Yuk, whoever would want to eat bugs?"

"Spiders love bugs, my dear!!"

"Yuk, oh no!"

"The spider is made in a way that makes him enjoy bugs. On the underside of the spider's head are two sharp, pointed structures. The spider uses these to catch the insect".

"Wow, Neat!!" "It then paralyzes the insect, and makes the insect's tissues into liquid and then sucks it into its stomach. So you see that the spider works very, very hard to get food".

"Boy Grandma, I sure am glad I'm not a spider".

I looked and looked for Mr. Spider, but I could not find him.

One day, we were outside having a barbeque at Grandma's house. I was playing near the nut tree and I looked up. "What do you think I saw?"

There was Mr. Spider spinning another web.

I was so excited, "Hello Mr. Spider", I called.

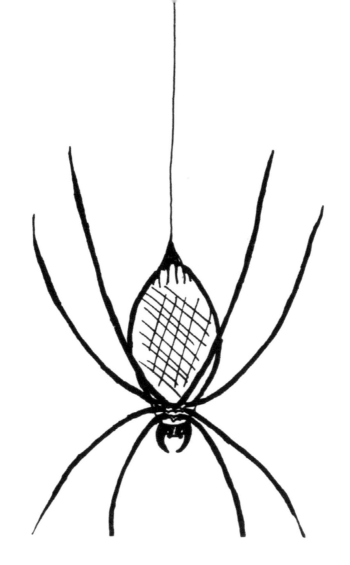

Printed in the United States
By Bookmasters